DEDICATION

To my loved ones.

TABLE OF CONTENTS

INTRODUCTION

Clearly, men and women are different in nature and this has probably fascinated human beings since time immemorial. Vast volumes of research and literature exploring these differences have been compiled and it seems like more is yet to come.

As much as these differences are natural, and welcomed, men and women, seem to have a hard time communicating in a common language when in romantic relationships. This often leads to conflict, quarrels, and doubts in regard to whether or not they have made the right choice in choosing their partner.

Yes, men and women are completely different in their approaches when it comes to how they perceive and approach relationships, but I am writing this book to help clarify the nature of their differences and provide you with a better understanding of how these differences can be mitigated.

As I have mentioned, these differences are welcomed and we should all learn how to appreciate them and stop expecting our partners to feel and act in the same way we do. Relationships have never and will never survive without mutual understanding and consideration. This is not to say that relationships with mutual understanding and consideration do not fail, but this is a prerequisite for any successful relationship, without which you are headed for imminent ruin.

Without the effort to understand one another and find a middle ground that works for both parties, relationships become an intense battlefield and a fight for control that neither of you knows how to navigate; a destructive battle that no one ever really wins.

There is no one-size-fits-all approach to relationships, but there are approaches you can take to guarantee yours has the highest possible chance of success. If you have been feeling tired and powerless in your quest to create a strong, healthy relationship, then this book is just what you need.

This book does not contain dry, dubious, tips and techniques for building relationships, which are basically manipulations in most cases. Instead, this book will attempt to get to the core of your relationship, establish a strong foundation, and leave you feeling stronger and healthier than ever.

My goal is to touch at your heartstrings and take you through a soul-searching trip that will have you looking into the nature and essence of your relationship, to find gentle solutions for most of the problems you may be experiencing with your partner.

Simply taking the time to read this book will have a huge impact on the state of your relationship. I highly recommend, not only reading the text but actually completing the exercises shared here. I personally love the ideologies in this because they really do yield the desired results. I have been receivingimmensely positive feedback from my clients, all testament to the great results realized by applying the approaches and principles contained herein.

I, therefore, want to encourage you to stick it out, no matter how difficult the exercise may seem or how far out of your comfort zone they may feel. In fact, if you feel an internal resistance, it should be a sign that you are making progress; change never comes easy, but it is always worth it.

Remember, you and your partner can work through just about anything as long as you are both willing to try, apply the same kind of effort, and refrain from destroying each other or yourselves. At the very core, most relationships, despite their uniqueness, are successful for the same reasons and in this book, I seek to share those principles and approaches with you. So, if you appreciate information that will not only make you smarter but also impart an ability to make better judgments, then this book is definitely worth the read.

WE ARE SO DIFFERENT, WHAT FOR?

Tell me honestly, what did you expect from this chapter? That, like in most books covering this subject, I will begin by explaining the nature of men and women, emphasizing the differences. I should prescribe that men are meant to be strong, while women – gentle and kind. Has that information ever helped anyone? No. Does it irritate everyone? Yes. So, I'm not going to focus on that. I perceive my readers as adults, who are capable of making their own behavioral choices.

We will try to deviate a little from common stereotypes and give both men and women a level playing ground on which each party will be responsible for their actions, or lack thereof, regardless of gender.

No one owes you anything

This is the very first thing we need to realize when we get into a relationship; your partner does not owe you a thing. They are with you of their own free will and will act of their own free will. Everything that makes up your relationship's dynamic depends on the personal arrangement you have as a couple. Preconceived thoughts about who should be who only lead to unnecessary expectations that are disastrous for any relationship. We will talk about expectations later on.

Of course, fundamentally, men and women are different, and it may be true that from an evolutionary perspective, we do have different needs. But I do not want to place too much emphasis on this because, first of all, this endless talk of gender differences does not lead to any material solutions. Second, it eliminates the need for both men and women to take responsibility for their erroneous ways because "that's just how I am wired".

As a side note, the best way to look at these differences is realizing that they actually make life fuller, they allow both men and women to learn and borrow from each other, and allows us to grow into the best versions of ourselves.

The very first step to a healthy relationship is to look at your partner as a human being rather than what their gender is because it is from such an outlook that we begin to form unhealthy expectations based on perceptions and stereotypes we have been fed since we were kids.

Falling prey to these stereotypes leads to a sense of entitlement from both men's and women's perspectives. You start to assume that because you are my woman you owe me this or that, or because you are my man I am entitled to this and that, otherwise you have failed in your role.

These stereotypes give us a misconstrued perception of our partners rather than truly seeking out who they are as individuals and approaching them from a point of true understanding. They also blind us to the fact that no one in this world really owes you anything, whether you are in a relationship with them or not. Reject the sense of entitlement that comes with relationship/gender stereotypes and begin to look at your partner as an individual, then build from there. Understand that, despite our differences, both men and women are looking for the same thing. We are all looking for some satisfaction, partnership, dignity, love, affection, and self-fulfillment in our relationships. We want our partners first to acknowledge us as the unique individuals we are before they can acknowledge us as men or women.

From here you need to admit the fact that your partner is, if you called a spade a spade, the person you have earned. You need them exactly as they are so that you can experience the necessary life lessons at that very stage in your life. This is called acceptance; embracing your partner as the unique individual that they are and focusing on their growth from that point on rather from a preconceived idea of who they are supposed to be.

LOVE IS ACTION

The meaning of the word "love"

The word love has numerous definitions, often used in different contexts, but the true meaning of the word is often vague and blurry. I will, therefore, take a crack and try defining love in the romantic context. True love in a romantic setting is an all-consuming emotion that takes over completely. It's not a goal to aspire towards or a substance that depends on the other party's actions or inactions; it simply is, and cannot be contained or controlled.

Love, therefore, manifests itself on the outside in the form of actions and this allows us to become our best selves. It's an outward manifestation of our emotions. It's a moment of faith in which we decide with all of our hearts that we want, above everything, to be with the objects of our affection, our partners.

This sounds beautiful and, it is, but unfortunately, we have been fed a false narrative about love, primarily by Hollywood and telenovelas. We have been led to believe that when we meet 'the right one' they will immediately fall in love with us as well, the world will brighten, and everything will, on that day, suddenly fall into place, like finding the missing piece of a puzzle.

However, the truth is, true love is complicated, it gets messy. True love is based on active thoughts, decisions, and actions to stick to with your significant other and finding ways in which you can fit into the chaos of each other's lives. It is knowing all the ways in the world that you two are imperfect, but still feeling that you make a beautiful unit and that you wouldn't rather be with anyone else.

Love is not simply a feeling, it is two souls intertwined, two bodies coming together to form one. It's not just about being with someone who buys you stuff, who takes you out on dates or kisses you, or who makes you laugh, it's the feeling of appreciating your partner as part of you, even closer than family.

Love is actually a challenge, it's meeting someone who challenges you to be better than you have ever been. It's finding someone that you want to fight battles for and someone who is willing to fight your battles alongside you. It's not finding that your life is now full, it's discovering that your life was already full as it was, but their presence in your life has somehow made it feel complete.

It's the feeling of that person's fingers interlocked in yours as you grow old. It's sharing your life, sharing experiences, sharing family, and maybe even children of your own. It's the feeling of forever, no matter how hard that is to visualize, and realizing that there is no one else you would rather have spent your life with on this rock.

But love also comes with messiness, fear, confusion, insecurities, and still never giving up on one another but instead pushing each other to carry forward and to learn from one another. It's a life well-lived, a life fully experienced.

So, you see, my friend, love is not just a feeling, it's a relentless commitment that you make every day you're alive. It is a decision, a choice, growth, a movement towards each other no matter what obstacles this world attempts to throw your way, despite all the things that may try to break you down, and despite how the times may try to force you to walk away from one another.

Despite life's impermanence and despite how limited our time on earth is, love is the conviction that you believe in each other and that you choose to give whatever little time you have to this one person. Love is Action.

EMOTIONAL INTIMACY IS THE KEY

What is emotional intimacy?

Sure, the strongest relationships are built on elements such as love, respect, and trust. All this sounds lovely, but what most of us fail to understand is that in order for these elements to exist and thrive in a relationship, one crucial ingredient must exist, which is *Emotional Intimacy*. This is because any relationship built on an emotionally secured bond is almost unbreakable.

Most people tend to focus on the physical and material aspects of a relationship, but so many potentially great relationships have failed simply because the couple overlooked the importance of emotional intimacy. While it is possible to intentionally focus on the physical and material while overlooking the emotional aspects, this approach is unsuitable for any relationship that you hope will stand the test of time.

If are looking to make your relationship last you need to prioritize building the emotional bond between you and your partner. Not only does emotional intimacy in a relationship strengthen your union but it has also been proven to be vital for the individual wellbeing of the parties involved.

Stressors, tight schedules, changes, mental preoccupation, physical distance... so many things can cause a rift between ourselves and our partners, causing us to become distant and withdrawn. It is imperative, however, to note that the things that cause us to lose touch with our partners don't always have to be negative.

Even positive changes and personal achievements could be the reason why we lose that emotional connection with our loved ones because they tend to come with deep investments that have nothing to do with our partners. For example, promotions at work, having to be there for a friend during tough times, new interests and hobbies, etc.

Maintaining emotional intimacy is, therefore, something that you have to monitor closely because it is quite easy to lose. The good news is, however, that is quite easy to establish and maintain emotional intimacy, and if you want to solidify emotional intimacy in your relationship, here are a few tips on how you can go about that.

Break down your walls

This is the very first step towards emotional intimacy; there can be no emotional intimacy in a relationship if you and your partner are both on guard. Emotional intimacy begins when both parties trust one another despite their weaknesses, vulnerabilities, and fears. It therefore folows that you and your partner should both break your walls down and let each other in.

You have to have trust in each other. The establishment of a strong emotional bond will only be underway when you have both shed off your armor and broken down the walls you have built around your hearts.

Discuss the past with an open mind

The past can be a sensitive subject, especially for new couples who are just embarking on their relationship. It may be extremely sensitive to talk about situations that broke your heart and that molded you into who you are today, but this is an important aspect of building emotional intimacy because it is a show of trust and faith in your partner and it also forms a basis of understanding in the relationship.

By sharing exactly what you've been through without holding back any information, your partner will be able to understand why you behave and react the way you do to different situations. You may be wondering why it is important to discuss the past with your partner in the first place; should not the past stay in the past?

Well, that would be the most ideal situation but, the truth is, no matter how much we try, our pasts and the people in it continue to influence us. The past influences our values, our beliefs, our characters, our behaviors, our reactions, etc., and it is important for your partner to understand, intimately, exactly where you are coming from.

Acknowledge their pain

Our painful experiences have had much more of an impact on us than our happy/positive experiences. As you share your own experiences, make it a point to try and understand your partner's experiences, acknowledge every bit of information and internalize it. To build an emotionally strong union you need to be deeply aware of all the words, actions, instances, etc., that make them feel scared, hurt, or unloved.

Couples with an emotionally strong bond understand how to treat their partners in order for them to feel safe. They know the right words to use, what actions to take, and how to approach them because they understand them on a deeply emotional level. They feel what their partner feels and they can almost accurately predict what their partner is thinking in different situations and this kind of connection allows for growth, healing, and a stronger connection between the parties.

Understand what makes them come alive

Besides having an intimate understanding of the things that cause your partner pain, you also need to understand the things that make them come alive; those things that light a fire in their belly, this way you will also have a clear picture of who they are and who they can be at their very best. This will guide you on what to do in order to make them happy and how to lift their spirits when they are going through challenging times. This will also inform you on how to keep them motivated and working towards their own goals and desires for truly sustainable happiness.

There is no emotional intimacy, not any sustainable intimacy at least when couples are not being completely sincere and honest in everything that they do. You have to be absolutely genuine when expressing care towards your partner and, this should not be too difficult to do if you truly love them, right?

Let them know that they do not need to doubt your words or intentions; let them trust you by simply sharing your true self. Remember, human beings have intuitions that tell them when something is not quite adding up. If you are not being genuine in your words and in your actions your partner may pick up on this and it may cause them to withdraw, effectively destroying any chance for emotional intimacy you may have had.

This is possibly the most important pointer I will be sharing here; let yourself have fun. Emotional intimacy is more likely to exist amongst couples who regularly make each other laugh. Humor has also been said to be a contributing factor in long-lasting relationships and most people will agree that they do not get tired of being in the company of people who amuse them. While the subject of emotional intimacy may sound serious, and it is, humor and laughter do have a way of softening the heart and prompting us to shed off our armor.

Building emotional intimacy with your partner means laying yourself bare for another person to see, and this can be a very scary thing to do. However, if you truly love your partner and you truly want to create a strong, long-lasting bond with them, you need to muster the courage to let them see your soul. So, take that leap of faith today and leave no stone unturned.

This short psychological test will help you analyze how things are going in your relationship. Just write *YES* or *NO* next to each statement. Write the first thought that comes to your mind, do not overthink.

1. I can easily list 3 things that inspire me the most in my partner.

2. When we are not together, I often think of him/her in the very best light.

3. I regularly find ways to tell him/her *'I love you'*.

4. I often show tenderness – stroke or kiss my partner.

5. My partner respects me very much.

6. I feel loved, very well taken care of.

7. I feel understood and accepted.

8. My partner thinks I'm sexy and attractive.

9. He/she turns me on.

10. There is a fire and passion in our relationship.

11. Romance is definitely a part of our relationship.

12. I am very proud of my partner.

13. My partner is proud of and happy about my achievements in life.

14. I can easily tell why I chose that person.

15. If I started all over again, I would choose him/her again.

16. We almost always hug before falling asleep.

17. When one of us comes back home, we are glad to see each other.

18. My partner appreciates what I do for our family.

19. My partner generally likes my character.

20.Our sex life is generally satisfying.

If you have everything *'Yes'*, congratulations, you are a super couple! It should be like that in a healthy, happy couple relationship.

If you have less than 5 *'No'*, your relationship needs attention and improvement.

If you have more than 5 *'No'*, I recommend seriously addressing the relationship issues.

WHAT DETERMINES HAPPINESS IN A RELATIONSHIP?

Are you willing to go "into depths" with your partner?

The desire to dig deep and go 'into depths' is a major determinant of whether your relationship will live or die. Every one of us has our own 'black holes'; fears, complexes, childhood traumas, and so on. Entering into a truly close relationship with another means that these injuries would be revealed. And here the decisive moment is whether you are ready to accept one another as you are and mutually work on developing yourselves. However, most relationships' downfall is that some people are only seeking pleasure from the relationship and are afraid to go into depths, to those truly dark places where our demons hide.

It gets to a certain point where these individuals are constantly changing partners, and this can go on forever. It will always seem to these people that they deserve more but, the truth is, as long as you are looking for someone to always make you happy, you will never last long in any relationship you initiate. Relationships are not just for pleasure, at least not for that alone; they are for working towards mutual development, growth, and transformation.

Note, I am not encouraging you to approach your relationship as a project, complete with milestones and deadlines. No, this is a destructive approach that will have your partner feeling suffocated and, most probably, trigger rebellion and the collapse of your relationship.

Rather, talk to your partner about the growth and transformation you would like to make together and begin this journey mutually. Be patient and let your partner evolve at a pace they are comfortable with and, as long as they are willing to try, compromise, and make actual efforts towards the betterment of themselves and your relationship, you can only get better with each passing day.

If you truly love the person you are with, you should never try to change them. Trying to change another person is egotistical; you are trying to change another person's essence to better fit the selfish narrative of your relationship you are trying to form. You should never put a person you love through the guilt of having to feel as though who they are is not good enough.

Sure, you can communicate and explain that there are better ways of being and that there is room for growth and improvement, but at each stage of their growth process, they should always feel accepted in the relationship, just as they are. You cannot force your partner to act in a manner that is unnatural for them just to make you happy. You are engaging a human being with a history, vulnerabilities, and limitations and you can't expect to snap your fingers and make them a totally different person. It is a selfish and unrealistic expectation.

In relationships, it is much better to understand and forgive rather than trying to manipulate the other party into being what you want them to be. Isn't that the whole point of unconditional love? Understand that your partner has imperfections and accept their shortcomings and flaws; remember that you have your own too.

We can inspire growth, but we can never force it. So, again, as long as your partner is willing to grow with you, as long as they are making effort towards the betterment of the relationship and each other, then that's all we can really ask of them. Ifyou find that you don't have the patience to walk with them through their growth process, I'll be brutally honest here... you are better off walking away from the relationship. Here are several reasons why trying to change your partner is a bad idea.

No one changes unless they want to

No matter how much you try, no one can truly change unless they want to. You cannot force a fish to climb a tree, it has to evolve in its own time to even be able to stay out of the water, and you can't rush this process. In the same way, you cannot force a person to be anything they have no interest in becoming. So, again, focus on inspiring change, not shoving it down their throat.

Focus on controlling what's within you

As I said, you have your own flaws and imperfections. Have you considered that maybe your partner isn't the problem? It's a possibility. Perhaps you have the wrong perspective on things and you may be surprised at how easy things can become with a simple change in your outlook or approach towards relationship problems.

Doesn't necessarily address the issue in the relationship

In most cases, relationship problems are offset by external factors and changing your partner won't necessarily change the environment that you have found yourself in. You may be directing your focus to the wrong place and changing your partner may end up being a moot exercise.

Stifle communication

When your partner feels like you are constantly judging and criticizing them, they may no longer feel the need to communicate with you anymore. They will no longer find it necessary to be honest with you and because communication and honesty are part of the vertebrae that make up the backbone of a relationship, once they are broken your relationship is crippled.

Generates resentment

If you are looking to preserve happiness and love in your relationship, you have to prevent any form of negativity from creeping in. The more you attempt to change your significant other the more distant and resentful they will feel about you, and if there is no more love in the relationship, you might as well kiss it goodbye.

Trying to change your partner only drives a wedge between the two of you. Healthy relationships are built on intimate and safe connections between you and your love and constantly trying to change only dilutes the feelings of safety, which discourages affection and intimacy between the two of you. So, I will repeat again; inspire change, don't force it.

Personal Transformation is a process

Personal growth and transformation are not something that happens in an instant, it takes time and patience. To build a perfectly healthy relationship demands your patience, resilience, and willingness to keep trying and growing to be better than you are. There is a reason why you are together, do you really want to quit when the next disagreement comes along? Do you want to give up on everything simply now or would you rather go further into the depths? I personally advocate for the latter.

Case Study

Acceptance and compromise

I had a middle-aged couple come into my office a while back and both of them were clearly waiting for the other person to change without really putting any effort into their transformation. The husband complained that he has been miserable for years now and that the wife wouldn't let give him any kind of space; he felt as though he was suffocating. On the other hand, the wife complained that the husband had friends over almost every weekend and never considered her needs; she felt like she was alone.

My solution, in this case, was unconventional, but simple. If you are waiting for your partner to change, you should begin by accepting who they are as an individual. When your partner feels unappreciated, disliked, and criticized, they will be extremely resistant to change. They will end up feeling under siege and only sink deeper to protect themselves.

As opposed to focusing your energy on criticizing your partner and pointing out their faults, remind yourself of their admirable qualities and share that with them. Change your perspective and become genuinely interested in understanding them and why they do and see things the way they do. Once you have grasped where they are coming from, be open to, not only accepting their uniqueness and your differences but actually accepting them.

Note, we are not talking about serious matters such as abuse or infidelity; these should obviously be nipped in the bud and addressed with the help of a professional. But if we are talking about smaller issues such as the one expressed by the couple above, you should seek to understand and accept your partner as they are. After this, you can then express how your partner's behavior is affecting and express to them why you may need them to do some things a little differently.

What our couple above didn't understand at first is that they were not having conflict over the amount of time they spent or didn't spend together. The underlying issue was actually the fact that neither was able to express what they needed in a non-blameful way. None of them was trying to understand what the other needed and why; they were both engrossed in what their individual needs were, it was a completely selfish dynamic.

Upon encouraging them to open up more and express why they each needed to spend their time in a certain way, it finally dawned on the husband that to his wife spending alone time together over the weekends with the family was a priority, it made her feel happy, fulfilled, and less lonely in the world. The wife also finally got that her husband is a social person and that spending time with close friends to simply talk to and bond over the weekend after a week of back-to-back working made him feel happy and fulfilled.

With this understanding of where each partner was coming from, they were able to hold on a little less tightly to each of their stances and come to a compromise. They decided to split the weekends; on the first and third weekends, the husband would have his time with his friends and on the second and fourth weekends they would spend alone time as a family. Everyone was happy, and no one felt manipulated or suffocated.

Couples that seek deep emotional connections have to understand how to be open and vulnerable in expressing themselves. In turn, they have to build a safe and understanding environment that allows for the expression of their deepest fears, hopes, and dreams without being judged for feeling how they feel.

Avoid being critical of your partner and seek to accept and understand them, then approach them from a point of understanding explaining why it is important to you that they alter their behavior. Criticism will only drive your partner into hiding and resistant to any kind of change you may be proposing. By consistently, approaching each other from a point of understanding and acceptance, however, you create a healthy bond that helps you navigate challenging moments and gives each of you a willingness to compromise for one another and meet in the middle every time.

Always be willing to ask sincerely and openly talk to each other about what is happening in the relationship. The main problem in most cases is the understatement, which leads to a lack of effective communication and emotional intimacy with your partner.

In such cases, you may even find that everything seems to be fine in a relationship, but there are constant underlying thoughts like: 'Is this my type of person?', 'Is he/she really suitable for me?', and 'Why is there no spark? The relationship is like a frozen swamp'. This is just about the lack of emotional intimacy. For a couple, it is crucial to talk openly about your feelings and to feel that your communication received with gentlenessand understanding.

HOW TO TALK ABOUT YOUR FEELINGS?

Talking isn't enough - learn to "convey" your thoughts and be heard

You should always understand that relationships are not born out of a vacuum; they are realized a couple comes together, each party with their own history, experiences, and expectations. These are two different people with completely different communication skills because it is something you acquire through exposure and it will always be different depending on the kind of environment your life has exposed you to.

The most common assumption about communication in relationships is that, as long as you are exchanging words with your partner, you are communicating. While speaking is indeed communication, if it is only about every day, surface-level topics like, *'How was work?'*, *'How's your project going?'*, *'How's your brother?'*, then you aren't really communicating about the most important things.

In this chapter, I want to take you through a more open and rewarding manner to communicate with your partner. Communication has the capacity to either make or break your relationship and you can improve the quality of your relationship immediately by implementing the communication skills we shall discuss here.

We have already mentioned that ineffective communication and understatement is what leads to most problems in our relationships. But how exactly should you go about speaking about yourself and your feelings? Here's a basic outline.

> ➢ Speaking of YOURSELF, use 'I' instead of 'You': *'I feel'*, *'My feelings are'*, *'I need to'* etc. Apply these as opposed to using words that impose blame on your partner such as, *'You did it wrong'*, *'You never listen'*, etc.

- ➢ Sincerely and openly talk to each other about what is happening without suppressing or hiding the thoughts, even in the hardest situations, for example: *'I think I fell out of love with you and fell in love with another men - I feel terrible, I don't know what to do'*.

If effective communication like this is not practiced, then love, warmth, emotional intimacy, and the spark the relationship once had simply dies.

Effective Communication Techniques

That is the outline of how you should approach all serious discussions you are going to have with your partner. It encourages openness from their part and, eventually, you can all understand where each of you is coming from and meet in the middle, no matter what conclusion the conversation leads to.

Nonetheless, here are a few more communication techniques you can employ for effective communication with your significant other.

Give your partner full attention

Whether your partner is telling you a deep dark secret of simply telling you a joke, give them your undivided attention. Your partner should feel that they have your undivided attention and this will send the message that you actually care about the information that they are sharing with you. Put the phone down and look them in the eye, nod, respond and maintain eye contact to show to acknowledge that you are listening. You can probably listen without doing all this but it makes your partner feel important and valued and that could mean the world to them.

Don't interrupt them

Have you ever noticed that interrupting another person is the quickest way to escalate a conversation? Well, this is more so for relationships because there are emotions involved. When communicating with your significant other, it is important for both of you to feel that you have adequate time to express yourselves without being cut short.

I understand that sometimes you feel the urge to squeeze in a statement here and there, especially when you are arguing, but I want to encourage you to train yourself to wait. Giving your partner the platform and patience for them to fully express themselves is an expression of respect and consideration and it will earn you the same and simultaneously deescalate the situation.

Speak face-to-face

Always try, as much as possible, to speak about important topics in person. Texting is certainly one of the worst ways to have important conversations or make decisions. Wait till you meet your partner no matter how tempting it feels to reach out and begin the conversation over the phone. Having important discussions in person allows both you to give each other your undivided attention, read facial expressions, and verbal cues. When your partner is right in front of you, it gives you the opportunity to fully understand each other and it is highly unlikely that anything will get lost in translation.

Discuss the little things

One of the most beautiful things in any relationship is when you and your partner can talk about both the little things as well as the big ones. You can share silly jokes, share stories about your week, have petty arguments, and still have serious discussions. When you are married, no topic should be out of bounds and there shouldn't be any topic too awkward or frightening to share.

Make physical contact

It is important that you maintain physical contact with your partner during discussions, especially the heated ones. Subtle contact with your partner, for example, holding their hand, stroking their arm, etc., releases oxytocin, the inducing hormone that creates a bond between romantic partners. The hormone also acts as a stress reliever that promotes cooperation between the two of you.

Last but not least, communication with your partner should be fun, it should be something you look forward to, not something you dread. This is a dynamic that must, however, be created by applying all the techniques discussed in this chapter. It takes work, effort, and a willingness from both parties, so encourage your partner today to embark on the journey to better communications with you.

Practical Exercise

Try the following practice: sit opposite each other and everyone sincerely and openly takes turns to say what he or she feels and what is in his or her soul. It may feel like you opened the old wound, pus spills out, it hurts. But it also heals afterwards.

To solve the most of the problems, it often turns out that all you needed was to open your heart and speak out. Even in the most complicated situations, the practice of sincere conversations may help a lot, and most times it is simply unfounded fear stopping you from communicating with your partner. If you are doing so, a great couple's therapy is taking place.

However, to make that practice work out correctly so that the conversation does not morph into mutual accusations, right at the beginning you need to 'set the mood'. Do this by starting the conversation with an affirmation that you trust each other; this will set up a friendly mood that leads to cooperation.

Keep the communication flowing, be willing to listen, don't be afraid to say you don't understand whenever you don't, make sure you are really paying attention to the message your partner is trying to send across.

UNDERSTANDING YOUR PERSONAL GOALS AND NEEDS

A lot of us go into relationships expecting the relationship to complete us. We assume that once we have met 'the right one' the stars will align, everything will suddenly make sense, and we will finally feel complete. While it is absolutely possible to find yourself in a relationship with your 'better half', this is not the right mentality to bring into your relationship.

It is my contention that, to give your relationship the best possible chance of success, you must first understand your own personal goals and needs. It is almost impossible to have a healthy and fruitful relationship if you don't even understand what you want for yourself. It is impossible to give someone else the best version of yourself when you are not even sure what that version is.

This will make you emotionally dependent on your partner, make you jealous and crazy, and lead to a lot of friction and conflict in your relationship. This will eventually turn your relationship sour and leave you both upset, confused, angry, and exhausted by the relationship. You will then begin to distance yourself and when feelings of isolation and loneliness begin to set in, even when you are with your partner, that's when you know your relationship is in deep trouble.

If any of this sounds familiar, whether in your current or past relationships, it may be about time to start focusing on and improving yourself before you can pursue any new romances or proceed with your current relationship.

This may sound very strange, having to work on yourself before giving yourself to a relationship, but I assure you that once you have started working on yourself, you will notice that you are becoming increasingly happier and confident. You will notice that you are becoming content with the person you are and you will radiate this energy to everyone around you, including your partner or potential suitor.

People are attracted to warm, confident, friendly people, with positive personalities, and your partner will love you more for it. It will simultaneously encourage them to work on themselves so that, at the end of the day, when you come together, you can each bring joy and happiness to the table and feed off of each other.

On the other hand, if you do not work on yourself before giving yourself to a relationship, you are more than likely to bring your baggage, confusion, uncertainty, and indecisiveness to the table, which will give birth to a myriad of negative qualities that will eventually suffocate your relationship from within. You will emit a sad, negative vibe and your partner will pick up on this and adopt a similar vibe or, even worse, be repelled by it.

Not only will you love yourself more if you work on your own wants and needs before getting into a relationship, but it will actually make your love life when you do find it or resume it, much sweeter. You will be happier and more positive in the relationship and this will be emotionally rewarding to both you and your partner. Here are a few compelling reasons why you need to take the spotlight off of your love and shed it on yourself for a moment.

How to identify your own needs:

Treat yourself with love

This is the very first thing you should do when you embark on the journey to identify your needs; you need to treat yourself lovingly, believe me, you deserve it. The world is a harsh enough place for you to be fighting wars within yourself. If your relationship with yourself is not great, it is likely that you are going to ignore your own desires, which is unhealthy for yourself as well as your relationship.

Make yourself a priority and listen to what you want and need, not just in love, but in every aspect of your life. If you feel that you want/ need something, then make no compromise and be resolved to go after it. If, however, you feel hesitant about something, find out why and do not put yourself in any situation that compromises your happiness and wellbeing.

Discover your Interests

When you begin focusing on yourself you will begin to discover hobbies and activities that truly interest you and make you happy. Take the time to engage in things that set your soul on fire and, for a moment, ignore all those that you engage in just to 'fit in'. Take time to do things that you genuinely enjoy and you will begin to feel happier both externally and internally.

Live healthily

Make an effort to lead a healthier lifestyle by monitoring your diet and engaging in exercise and sports. Set healthy milestones and track your progress. A healthy lifestyle contributes to one's mental wellbeing. This is not magic; studies have found that exercising actually releases dopamine in the brain, a feel-good hormone that improves one's mood and leaves you feeling strong and confident as you go about your day. Dedicate yourself to living healthy, eating healthy, and exercising regularly for a happier, more fulfilling life.

Focus on your definition of success

Society and the world already have a general definition of success but we need to understand that we are all different and we cannot all fit under a single, blanket definition of what success is. Define success for yourself and set goals and reasonable milestones around that definition. Focus all your energy and attention on the achievement of those goals and the realization of your vision. Once you do this you will find yourself in full control of your life. You will find yourself living a life of passion and power, which will leave you completely satisfied with the state and direction of your life.

Choosing yourself, your own needs, and your own happiness can be considered in some circles to be an act of selfishness but, in reality, it is quite the opposite. Think about it; if everyone in the world was at their happiest, would not the world be a better place overall?

The same applies for relationships; if you focus on yourself before giving yourself to one, you bring blissful joy with you that you are then able to share with your partner rather than being emotionally dependent and bleeding your relationship and partner because you expect to draw fulfillment from the union rather than from within.

Always remember, happiness and fulfillment should really be emanating from within you, so take the time to work on yourself first. Encourage your partner to do the same if you are already in a relationship and when you have both established great relationships with yourselves, come together and share your joy.

How to identify your needs in terms of relationship:

A lot of us did not receive any instructions on how to identify what we need from our romantic relationships, which is why we find ourselves with partners that we may indeed love, but with whom we are not compatible.

In the previous section, we have spoken about identifying your personal wants and needs as well as the importance of doing so before entering into a relationship. In this final section of the chapter, we will be discussing an equally important subject; how to go about identifying your wants and needs in a relationship. Let's get to it.

Do your homework

Have a clear vision of the kind of life you want to lead and then seek out a romantic partner who has a similar vision as yours. This will deter future conflict and disappointments because having a partner with whom you are in sync with will allow you to devise a mutually satisfying plan of action when it comes to the direction that your relationship and life together will be taking.

Identify and respect your values

For example, if you only feel comfortable when you are independent, you need to find a partner who understands this and who is willing to give you the kind of space you need. If you value trust above everything else in a relationship, you will need to choose a partner who demonstrates reliability and honesty. Going against your values and selecting a partner who does not share or, at least, respects them will only lead to future disappointment and frustrations.

Ensure flexibility

Control and rigidity have no place in a healthy relationship. Therefore, finding a partner who is willing to be flexible both in their thought process and in their actions is absolutely crucial. Life together will sometimes demand a compromise either from yourself or from your partner. This is a two-way street and you should find a partner who is willing to make healthy compromises just as much as you do.

Select a team player

Even when you take the above measures, issues and problems will always arise in relationships; this is quite normal. You, therefore, need to find a partner who is willing to collaborate with you in the resolution of any and all issues that may arise. A partnership between yourself and your significant other will give you the support necessary in finding critical and mutually satisfying solutions in your relationship.

FOUR PILLARS THAT HOLD THE RELATIONSHIP

Numerous factors determine the success of any relationship and it is quite possible that if we were to list these factors the list would almost be infinite. However, there are those crucial ingredients that carry the most weight in a relationship; these are the pillars of the relationship and if these pillars are strong, the chances of your relationship's success increase exponentially.

The four pillars are *Finance, Children, Sex and Core Values*. You need to talk openly about these factors and reach a consensus about how each of these spheres is going to be handled within your relationship, otherwise, they could morph into major points of conflict that could lead to a potentially irreversible fallout. Let's have a look at each of these pillars and the best way to approach each one.

Money

A lot of couples find it difficult to discuss finances with their significant others openly. It could be because they are embarrassed by the debt they have accumulated, sometimes due to their unhealthy spending habits, and other times because they just aren't happy with the amount of money they make. These are all very understandable reasons for apprehension in sharing the state of your finances with your partner, but you need to ask yourself how you are expected to plan any kind of future with your significant other if you never discuss money matters with them.

Being open about both your finances will allow you to set mutual financial goals such as retirement funds or the kids' tertiary tuition fees and allow you to support one another in the pursuit of your individual goals. Be open with your significant other, even if you are ashamed of the fact that you struggle with basic money management or that you have a poor credit history.

In all fairness, these are matters that your partner deserves to know about you so that you collaboratively come up with a plan that will not only guarantee your financial security moving forward but also bring harmony within the relationship. To make things a little more interesting, celebrate each financial victory.

For example, the clearing of a debt, hitting a savings target, making a major purchase such as a home. The celebration doesn't have to be grand, but it will really allow you to enjoy the completion of a milestone that you have worked on and completed together, which will encourage you to keep up the effort and continue securing your financial future together.

Children

Kids are a blessing and a joy in any relationship and could lead to increased love and warmth in the home, but they can also be a major point of conflict if you and your partner are not on the same page. Bringing up children together requires supportiveness, cooperation, and mutual involvement.

Not only does a cooperative collaboration in raising the kids lead to a stronger relationship between you and your partner, but according to studies, a healthy father-mother parenting collaboration also plays a major role in the brain development of children. Children tend to thrive in environments where the father and mother are providing consistent parenting as a team. The reason behind this is that it makes the children feel safe and secure without which they are more likely to act out, creating a vicious cycle of frustration and anger.

In parenting, learn how to support each other and, when decisions are made, the children need to know that they have been made in agreement by both parents. Always solve problems together and only after you have truly discussed the matter and agreed on the best course of action. Never speak ill of one another, especially in front of the kids; they only need to hear about the strengths you see in each other, not your weaknesses.

Team parenting ultimately creates peace within the relationship and it leads to the upbringing of healthier, happier children. It, however, can only be done if both parties are willing to work together, so set your pride aside, abandon all notions that you know better that your partner, and be willing to work collaboratively with your significant other for the greater good.

Sex

No matter how much we want to shy away from the topic, sex is an integral part of any relationship; sex and relationships go hand-in-hand. Not enough is said about the importance of sex in relationships, but all I know is that a healthy sex-life greatly enhances relationships and prolongs them, sometimes even perpetually.

There is no rule that dictates that sex has to happen in a specific measure or frequency but, the more it happens, the better you will both feel about yourselves and about the relationship. With the same logic, lack of or, minimal physical intimacy, takes from the relationship and snuffs out the spark and thrill it once had.

You and your partner need to talk about your sexual needs and desires and, you may feel a little shy doing it, but it is important to learn early on whether you are sexually compatible. Sexual incompatibility has long been known to be one of the biggest reasons for discord in long term relationships, so hiding your true needs and desires from your partner now is only be prolonging the inevitable.

Also, you should keep in mind that sex is not simply about orgasms, so broaden your perception of the subject. Sometimes sex is about emotional intimacy and bonding, connection, sensation; it's an act of love that deepens the connection you already have with your significant other, ultimately strengthening the relationship.

As an added bonus, sex also improves your health by exercising your cardiovascular system, enhancing your immune system, and acting as a stress reliever.

Core Values

Everyone has those fundamental beliefs and values that make them unique. Most of these values have been ingrained in us since our childhoods, imparted on us by our parents and the immediate environment. Some of these values and beliefs we picked up along the way from our observations and experiences. Either way, our core values affect the choices and decisions we make in regard to career, religion, politics, lifestyle, and practically every other aspect of our lives.

We are all quite comfortable making decisions that feel right to us and that align with our beliefs and values and when we go along with a decision that goes against those valueswe end up feeling unhappy, uncomfortable, and even guilty. Note, however, our core values have a capacity to change as we learn, grow, and evolve as individuals. However, it is unlikely that anyone could sustain a happy relationship with an individual with conflicting core values.

You could decide to change your values in a relationship to match your partner's, but ensure that you are not doing this as a compromise of your own deeply held convictions, but rather because you have learned that the new line of thought you are adopting is actually the right way. Otherwise, you will end up feeling compromised and unauthentic within your relationship, which may eventually lead to its collapse and your fallout.

Spend some time getting to know yourself, understand what values, beliefs, and convictions you hold dear and then determine what values and beliefs you are looking for in a partner.

1. Money

- What is our family income made up off?
- How are our financial reserves formed?
- What are our financial perspectives?
- Do we count on help from relatives?
- How and where willwe store money?
- Do we have a separate budget or a common one?
- How will we share the expenses?
- What is our relation to unplanned purchases?
- How will we plan serious purchases?

2. Children

- At what age, in your opinion, is it better to have children, and why?
- How and for what could we panish the child?
- What to do with childhool fears?
- How would we choose a school?
- How to raise a future leader?
- What is more important to develop, intelligence or feelings?
- How much freedom does a child need?
- Should we stay together for the kids?

3. *Sex*

- What do you enjoy most during love making?
- What are your innermost fantasies?
- What turns you on?
- Can a wife's attitude to sex affect her husband's feelings for her?
- Are experiments acceptable and desired in our sexual life?
- How often do we need to have sex?
- Would we watch pornography together?
- What do you like more, kissing or hugging?
- What type of men/women do you consider the sexiest?

4. *Core values*

- Are you satisfied with the way you communicate in a couple?
- Do you have a feeling that you understand your partner, and he/she understands you?
- Has it ever happened that you deliberately lied to your partner?
- Do you have enough time to spend together only?
- If you had the opportunity to spend more time together, how would you handle it?
- Do you have any goals, plans for this year? How would you implement them?
- For what things in your life do you feel grateful?
- For what things in our relationship are you thankful to me?

NEGATIVE BELIEFS

In the sphere of love and relationships, a lot of negative beliefs and attitudes exist. Just like gender stereotypes and preconceptions, these negative beliefs have been force-fed to us since we were young. For example, *'There are no good men left'*. You have such beliefs in your subconscious, and they definitely have an impact on your life. Our beliefs play a major role in how we approach life, how we view ourselves and the world at large. Our beliefs are not always reality, but they do influence how we view reality.

One of the most common negative beliefs the world has imposed on us is that there is a perfect partner and a perfect relationship waiting for us out there. Due to this fairytale narrative, we have been fed, we end up feeling unfulfilled in our relationships when we find that our partners are not perfect or at the first instance of conflict. We begin to cultivate the idea that our partner is below our standards and that the life you are living is far from perfect and, therefore, not a life deserving of you. What a terrible lie we have been fed.

Sure, there are situations that are truly 'far from perfect'. For example, where there is abuse, disregard, and infidelity involved; these are situations that need urgent attention and, if it comes down to it, these are situations that would warrant separation and even a break-up. Notwithstanding, no relationship, nor partner, will ever be perfect and if you put your ego aside for a second, you would realize that you will never be the perfect partner either. We all have our imperfections.

This is not the only negative/false belief that exists in the relationship dynamic. Negative could be anything really and could be acquired through multiple avenues including our own observations and conclusions, words spoken to us by our elders, our history and experiences, from television, you name it.

Hypothetical scenario

For example, if my father abandoned me as a child, I may conclude that abandonment is part and parcel of the relationships dynamic; it's an eventuality simply waiting to happen. I may then begin to subconsciously attract partners who are likely to abandon me and therefore reaffirm my belief in the eventuality of abandonment in relationships. Similarly, if I find myself with a partner who doesn't abandon me, I will be the one to self-sabotage the relationship by withdrawing emotionally and possibly even abandoning them. This way I can subconsciously recreate the abandonment scenario so that my belief holds true.

Negative beliefs in relationships are, more often than not (perhaps all the time), fallacies. Whatever they may be, they need to be destroyed. The only way around this, however, is to replace these old negative beliefs with new ones. Who we are and who we are attracted to has more to do with who we are on the inside; it's a reflection of the beliefs and values we have held onto for years. If we want to change what we attract and who we are attracted to and consequently change our luck in relationships, we need to transform our beliefs.

Recognize that when we approach a relationship, we approach it in one of two ways; with empowering beliefs or limiting beliefs. I have, therefore, an exercise you can use to set aside your limiting/negative beliefs and pave way for a new, healthier, more successful relationship.

- ➤ Make a table of 2 columns.

- ➤ Write down all the negative thoughts and beliefs that you identify yourself with in the left column.

- ➤ For every negative belief come up with 4-5 positive ones and write it down in the right column.

- ➤ Revisit this table and add to it on a regular basis until you are certain you have exhausted all your negative beliefs about relationships.

Focus on rejecting every negative belief on the left and affirming within yourself very belief on the right.

HOW TO MAKE CHANGES HAPPEN

Change yourself, not your partner

We have already discussed this matter, but it is important that we emphasize even more on it. No real or sustainable change will ever happen from trying to change your partner. If something doesn't suit you, place all your energy into trying to change yourself as opposed to changing your significant other. Keep this in mind.

As we mentioned at the beginning of the book, your partner is like a message sent to you by the universe. They are exactly who you need at that very moment in your life and you do not need to abandon ship every time things appear challenging. You need your partner exactly as they are in order for you to learn from them.

We must go through these lessons/challenges in a relationship and how you conduct yourself in this test will set the pace, then your partner will evolve into what you need them to be 'naturally' at every stage of your relationship. At this juncture, I feel that it is important for you to go back and meditate on the reasons why you should never try to change your partner, then come back and proceed with the book, I'll wait...

Sometimes we deceive ourselves into believing that only when our partners conduct themselves in a certain way, we will feel satisfied in our relationship, so we keep making efforts towards trying to mold them into this image that we have in our minds of the perfect partner. As mentioned, this is selfish; you are dealing with a human being with a unique history, experiences, and expectations. They are not your project, they are your partner!

In most cases, trying to change another person in the relationship will only make matters worse. Simply because you think you know better than they do when it comes to how they should think, feel, and behave, you find yourselves in an endless cycle of quarrels and conflicts.

My assumption is that you are reading this book because you have a genuine interest in building a healthy, satisfying relationship. If that is true, then you need to place focus on changing yourself rather than your significant other. You need to look within and find out in which ways you may be contributing to the collapse of the relationship rather than placing all the blame on your partner.

It is important that you understand that both you and your partner have different perceptions of reality, that you both have unique personalities and different forms of expression. Demanding that your partner change is in itself disacknowledgment of their uniqueness and, if that is something you feel that you need to do, you need to ask yourself if you would have been better off dating/being married to yourself. Quite frankly, trying to change your partner says a lot more about you than it does about them.

How to begin the process of change

The process of changing yourself simply begins when you are motivated to put in the work on yourself. This begins by simply accepting that you are not perfect and acknowledging that, indeed, there may be contributions you are making in the relationship that are actually harmful. Facing yourself andcalling yourself out in this regard takes courage, but this is the first step towards making things right.

This decision to embark on the path of change is absolutely crucial because it essentially decides whether your relationship is going to survive or not and, if you are single at the time of this self-analysis, whether your subsequent relationships stand a chance.

It is normal to feel some hesitation when you are embarking on this process, it is scary and embarrassing to call yourself out because most human beings have a complex that tells them that they are perfect and that it is the rest of the world that is the problem. It is hard to admit that you have some toxic traits in a relationship and that, as much as the other party may share some of the blame, you may be playing a very significant role in your relationship's breakdown.

However, if you want with all of your heart to see your relationship succeed, or your subsequent relationships at that, you have to be willing to overcome this hesitation and embark on this journey of change. Once your partner sees you making strides towards your own betterment, not only will they be inspired to do the same, but they will be more receptive to any input you may have on how you believe they can contribute to the bettermentof your union. This is because you are not being critical. Rather, you are leading by example and showing them that there are better ways to be. Remember, inspiration, not force.

This way, you begin to create a deep, safe, non-judgmental bond that will lead to truly sustainable intimacy and, consequently, the success of your relationship.

Focus on the positives

During this process, refrain from viewing the negative side of your partner and remind yourself why you for them in the first place. What was it that drew you to them? Think of the qualities in them that inspire you and begin to look at them in that light alone; view them as the strong and resourceful individuals you knew them to be before you peeked into the abyss and saw some of their demons; before you realized that they were human after all.

When we focus our minds on our partners in this light, we are suddenly filled with the same warmth for them as we were when we first encountered them. We suddenly want to communicate and really understand them and build strongrelationships with them. Direct your mind to look for strengths, not weaknesses. This will give you time to focus on your own improvement, inspire them to do the same, and provide your entire relationship with the strength necessary for consistent action.

Take the full responsibility

In essence, there are 3 conditions in which people normally live: *Responsibility, Infantilism, or Overprotection.*

Infantilism

The infantile person is the one in whom immature behavior dominates, characterized by unwillingness to take the responsibility and make decisions independently,often lacking life goals and aspirations. That person is always a victim of circumstances, in his/her opinioneverything happens by itself or is done by others.

Overprotection

Overprotective people save or teacheveryone and everyone, or only the most lost ones, on their path.Their main desire is to be needed and feel their worth.

There is nothing wrong with empathizing, helpingin fairness and conscience, upholding the rights of those who, for some reason, cannot protect themselves, but with one caveat: without fanatical altruism and that should not be harmful for yourself.

It is quite common to find infantile and overprotective people together in a relationship. It is not bad or good, but the problem is that both of them will never realize their full potential in life if they continue 'playing their roles' for the rest of their lives.

Responsibility

The responsible person makes decisions and also corrects them according to changing circumstances, thinks more broadly and flexibly unlike the ones who do nothing. That is the only condition in which the inner freedom could exist.

The word "responsibility" is often understood and interpreted differently. Misinterpretation of the concept provokes a desire to escape from it.For many people, responsibility is associated with something truly unpleasant, a heavy feelingof a burden or a cross to bear on the shoulders. Othersbelieve that being responsible means meeting someone else expectations. The most common case is when people confuse responsibility with the guilt.

I am asking you to track your feelings while doing the next practical exercise. You may feel upset and even start to think that you are guilty of all the problems that have occurred in the relationship.Please note, when you decide to take responsibility, it does not mean that you are guilty.Taking responsibility is not the same as being guilty. Shake off the feeling of guiltiness, as it is the typical behavioral model of a victim. So be honest, but also remember to be kind and gentle with yourself in this exercise.

Your next practical exercise: *Accept the idea that everything that happens, occurs at your own request, desire, and assumption. Take full responsibility.*

Write down these points; how you feel about your relationship using the example of the statements below. It is important to use exactly the same formula. Pay attention and devote the time to this exercise; try hard to draw out all relevant information from within yourself.

Example:

1. 'I am not happy, because there is no romance in our relationship'.

2. 'I fully admit, that it is my responsibility. That situation happened due to ... (a lot of work, everyday routine, etc.)

3. 'I intend to change that situation the following way... '.

EXPECTATIONS KILL

Expectations kill your happiness and love

Showing your partner appreciation and love every day is the only way to protecting your relationship in the long-term. However, breakups, infidelity, breaks, and any other relationship bummers you can think for can still happen; unfortunately,nothing is promised in life or in love. However, doing your best to care for and nurture the love you have may give it more life than most relationships get these days, hopefully forever.

However, as you and your partner strive to preserve your relationship and do things for each other to keep each other happy and interested, let us remember the golden rule, *'Nobody Owes You Anything!'* That goes for your girlfriend, your wife, your husband, or your boyfriend, nobody!

Having expectations that your significant other should do certain things for you actually kills the willingness to do those things. Do not take the little things your partner does for granted, even when you have both delegated specific duties to each other. Always take the time every now and then to show them just how much you appreciate everything they do, even if it's by simply acknowledging that you have noticed their efforts.

If you ever find yourself out of creative ideas to show some appreciation to your partner, in this chapter I have gathered a few simple but great ideas you can borrow.

Practice words of affirmation

This is probably the most effective way to show the partner your appreciation. Encourage your partner and say nice words. Actually, I challenge you to take this up, as a rule, you practice in your relationship: *10 positive remarks for 1 negative remark.*

Regularly tell your partner just how much you care, tell them how much you love them, and how much you appreciate the little joys they have brought into your life simply by being who they are. Reject the notion that your partner should automatically know that you care; they need to hear those things you feel for them, so say them out loud and do it on a consistent basis.

Remember, however, that the most important aspect of saying words of affirmation is being genuine in what you are saying. If you are saying things simply to say them, your partner will pick up on this and it may plant a seed of doubt in their mind about how genuine you are as a person. So, don't fake it!

Also, you don't necessarily need to be Romeo or Alejandro to profess your love to your significant other, you simply need to be yourself, just be real. If you are not used to expressing yourself in words, here is your chance to practice, who knows you may even surprise yourself. Besides, you have nothing to lose.

Simple statements to get you started could be:

'I am so proud of you.'

'My love, I notice how hard you work for us, even when things are being tough. I need you to know that I appreciate you.'

'I am so lucky to have you in my life.'

'I am always here if you need me and I will support you any way I can.'

'I believe in you, you got this, you were made for this.'

'Wow, you look really good in that new outfit.'

Other Ways to Demonstrate Appreciation:

Notice the little things

As mentioned, simply because you have established a clear breakdown of roles and duties, doesn't mean that you shouldn't be grateful. For example, perhaps you load the dishwasher and your partner unloads it, or you mow the lawn and your partner trims the hedges, you can still show your appreciation for the things they do. For example, you can randomly say, *'Thanks for dinner dear, it's amazing'* or you could actually show appreciation by taking on a role they normally take up. You could tell them, *'No honey, sleep a little longer, I'll get the kids ready today'*.

Support their passions

You and your partner may have a lot in common, but since you are totally different individuals, it is unlikely that you will have the same passions. In most cases, you find that your partner is passionate about things that you have absolutely no interest in, but they somehow mean everything to the person you love.

Make it a point to give your time to pursue their passions, give them your support and even take part in some of their activities for moral support. If they are into health and fitness, go to the gym every now and then. If they are into pottery, attend some of their classes. If they love traveling, clear your schedule to visit new places with them. Having your support will mean everything to them and bring the two of you even closer as a unit.

Date your partner

Life can be difficult and as we grow older, the busier we seem to get. What we forget is that we were also preoccupied with matters relevant to us at the time we started dating our partners, but we somehow always made time to meet up and have a cup of coffee, to send flowers, watch a movie, or simply take a walk in the park. What changed?

Make time every week, no matter how things genuinely become, to come together and share an evening together. Use this time to truly catch up and reconnect; talk about your lives and really listen to each other. Wear something fancy every now and then and take your partner out for did, just like you did when you began. This is not only fun and keeps the fire burning in your relationship, but it makes your partner feel loved and wanted, and that could mean the world to them.

TODAY IS YOUR NEW WEDDING!

From here on out, your new life begins, you no longer have the same relationship you did yesterday. You are leaving the past behind and jumpstarting your relationship; this is a totally new place. But for this change to be truly sustainable, you need to have an open heart and an open mind; this is the only way you will create a new dynamic in the relationship and cultivate a healthy union.

If your hearts are still resistant to the practices and changes we have discussed above, then every bit of knowledge you have gained here as well as the renewal of your vows will all be futile and I am certain you don't want that. If your hearts are not committed to change, no amount of relationship advice, in this book or otherwise, will lead you to a happy and healthy relationship.

I also want to encourage you to create a strong friendship, look to each other as best friends before you are lovers, before you are a couple. Sharing a close friendship with your significant other is extremely vital for your relationship since emotional intimacy is definitely much more important for the success of a marriage than physical intimacy. Focus on creating a companionship in which you enjoy each other and honestly want what's best for one another.

Commit to the pursuit of growth both individually and as a couple and help each other reach your fullest potential both in your relationship and beyond it. Remember, never try to move forward alone, completely leaving your partner behind. In the same breathe, never threaten your partner with abandonment, no matter how rough things may get. You need to be each other's safe place, a place where you are always welcome, and a place you can always run to. You both need to feel that you indeed have a 'partner' in the fullest sense of the word; you both need to feel that someone indeed has your back no matter what.

Finally, in the spirit of renewal, you and your partner need to consistently monitor and evaluate your progress. Revisit the principles and approaches in this book and make sure you are sticking to them.

Also, regularly ask yourself, *'Would I like to be married to the kind of person I am today?'* If the answer is *'No'* there is clearly some work to be done, but if the answer is *'Yes'* then you are on the right track.

Time has passed, you have both evolved and changed, and you have probably even forgotten what you said at your actual wedding. Hopefully, after reading this book and taking part in all the exercises, you will become more confident and inspired enough to create new vows!

Even if you are not married yet, you definitely have promises you made to one another at the beginning of the relationships and this is the time to revisit them and renew them. This time, you will get to make more meaningful, more informed, more intentional, and more conscious vows.

When you are ready, sit across from each other and say your new vows with full attention and mindfulness. It's not a necessity, but I suggest that you do this exercise in a special place with a special ambiance to really give it the event some magnitude and importance in both your minds.

IN SUM

The truth is, when it comes to relationships, most of us are winging it. We get exhilarate by the early stages of the relationship, but as we move on to a more regular grind, personal baggage begins to become more visible in our partners. This eventually leads to disappointment, emotional withdrawal, hurt feelings, and just plain boredom and detachment from our significant others. Does this sound familiar? Creating and maintaining a happy relationship is certainly no walk in the park.

However, as we have seen in the course of this book, there is also no mystery to creating a healthy and happy relationship. Every successful relationship there is, despite its uniqueness, credits its success to the same principles, consideration, understanding, a willingness to try, positivity, consistent support, compromise, and a deep friendship.

You and your partner both have a say in where your relationship is heading; you are all equally responsible for your actions and inactions. To make a relationship work, therefore, demands effort from both parties, one is simply not enough. You must both be willing to meet halfway and work as a unit to make positive changes and become better with each day.

A healthy and happy relationship is one that is constantly growing and one that is constantly bringing out the best in you. You do not have to feel happy all the time, every relationship will experience rocky phases, but if you are both willing to learn and grow from the rough times and come out better than you were before, there will always be light at the end of the tunnel, and there will always be something beautiful to look forward to, and that is worth holding onto.

Apply the principles I have shared in this book and fully commit to incorporating them in your day-to-day life and your relationship. Encourage your significant other to join you on this journey and with effort on both your parts, you will give birth to a healthy relationship that will make both of you feel confident and supported, not just for a moment, but possibly for eternity.

Finally, once you have formed a healthy, happy dynamic, reach back and use the knowledge and wisdom you have acquired by helping younger, less experienced couples navigate their own journey of love. Let's make our world a more fulfilling world, one couple at a time. Love and Light!